MUSIC INSPIRED BY THE AMAZING GRACE

Contents

Artwork from the motion picture 'Amazing Grace'
© 2007 Bristol Bay Productions LLC. All Rights Reserved.

ISBN-13: 978-1-4234-5125-9
ISBN-10: 1-4234-5125-2

HAL•LEONARD®
CORPORATION
7777 W. BLUEMOUND RD. P.O. BOX 13819 MILWAUKEE, WI 53213

AMAZING GRACE
(My Chains Are Gone)

Words by JOHN NEWTON
Traditional American Melody
Additional Words and Music by CHRIS TOMLIN
and LOUIE GIGLIO

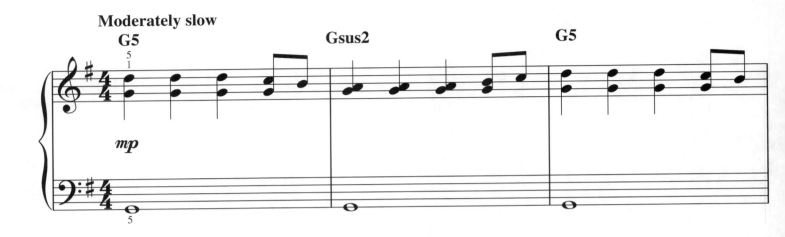

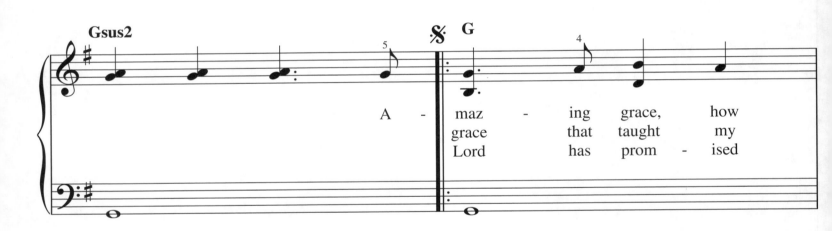

A - maz - ing grace, how
grace that taught my
Lord has prom - ised

sweet the sound, that
heart to fear, and
good to me, and His

saved a wretch like
grace my fears re -
Word my hope se -

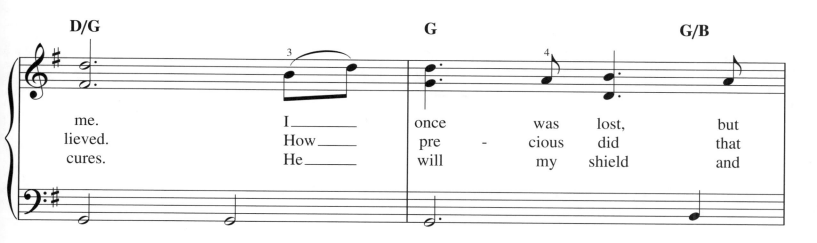

me. / lieved. / cures.

I ___ once was lost, but
How ___ pre - cious did that
He ___ will my shield and

To Coda

now I'm found, was blind, but now ___ I
grace ap - pear the hour I first ___ be -
por - tion be as long as life ___ en -

1.

2.

see. ___ 'Twas lieved. My chains are gone, ___ I've been set

free. ___ My God, my Sav - ior ___ has ran - somed

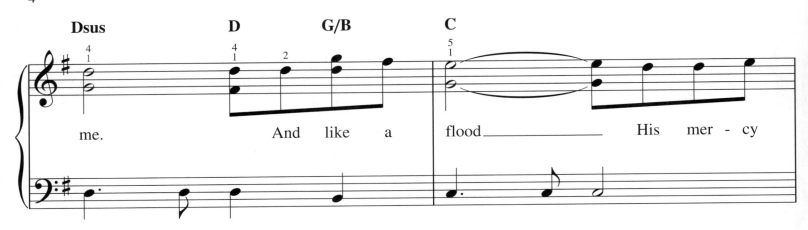

me. And like a flood_____ His mer - cy

rains_____ un - end - ing love,_____ a - maz - ing grace.

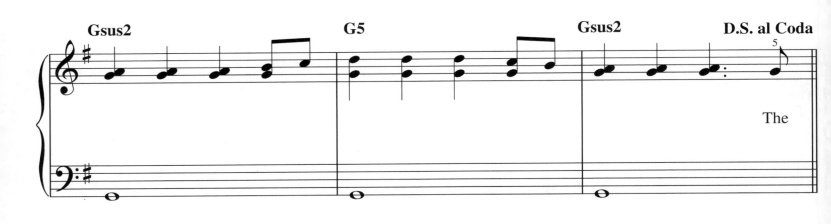

The

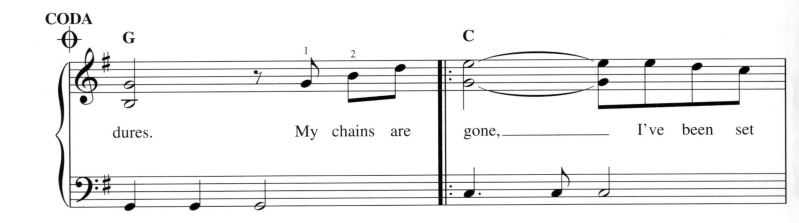

dures. My chains are gone,_____ I've been set

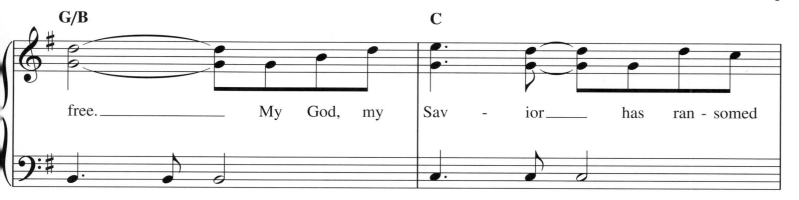

free._____ My God, my Sav - ior_____ has ran - somed

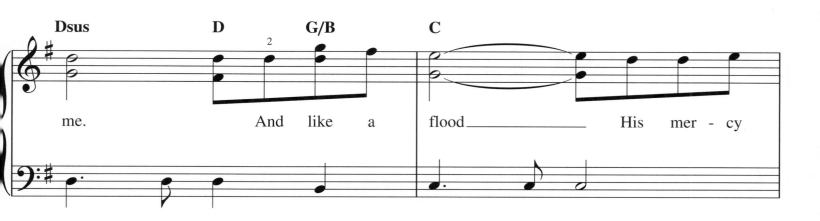

me. And like a flood_____ His mer - cy

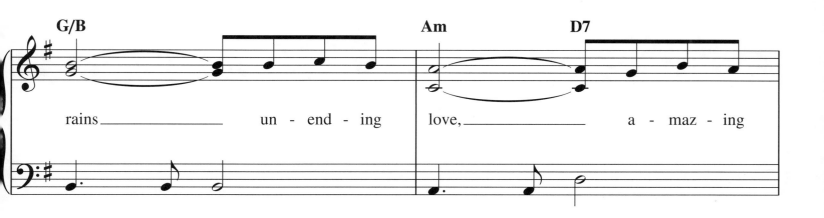

rains_____ un - end - ing love,_____ a - maz - ing

grace. My chains are | grace. The

earth shall soon dis - solve like snow, the sun for - bear to

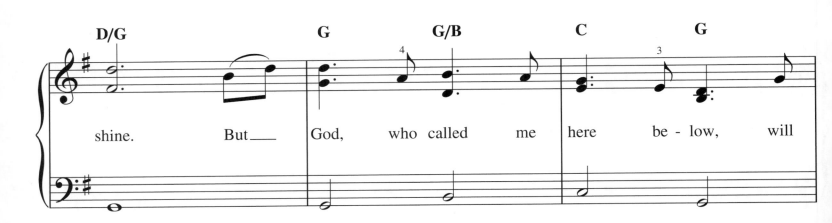

shine. But___ God, who called me here be - low, will

be for - ev - er mine, will be for - ev - er

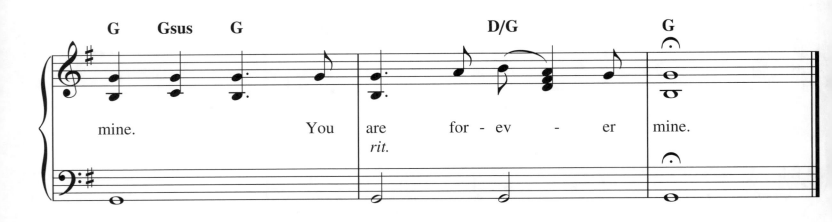

mine. You are for - ev - er mine.

rit.

IT IS WELL

Traditional
Arranged by JEREMY CAMP
and ADIE CAMP

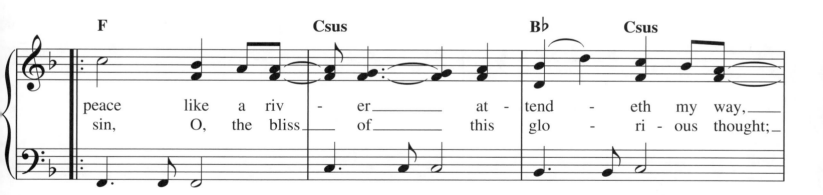

peace   like   a   riv   -   er_____   at - tend - eth   my   way,_____
sin,   O,   the   bliss_____   of_____   this   glo - ri - ous   thought;_

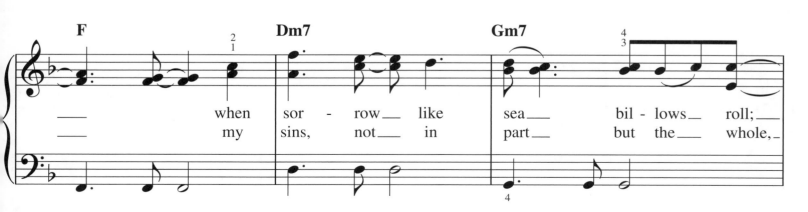

_____   when   sor - row_____   like   sea_____   bil - lows   roll;_____
_____   my   sins,   not_____   in   part_____   but   the_____   whole,_

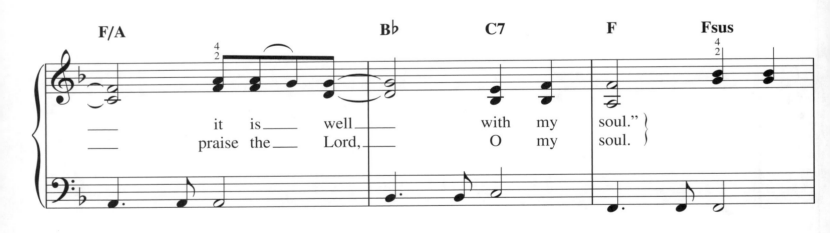

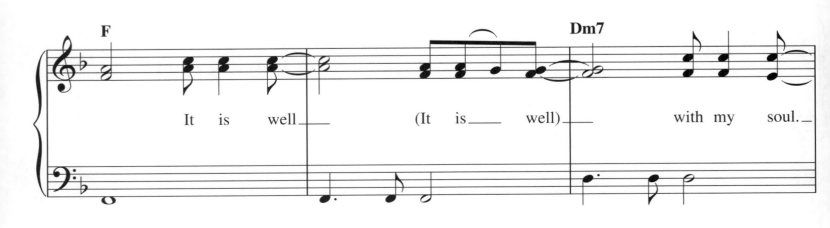

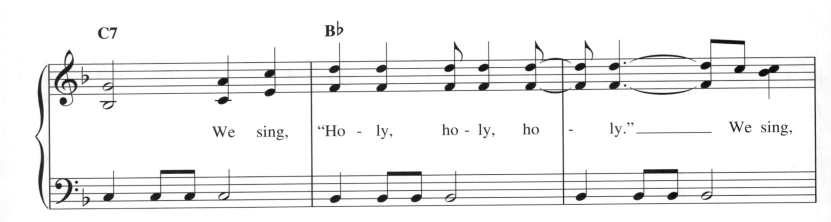

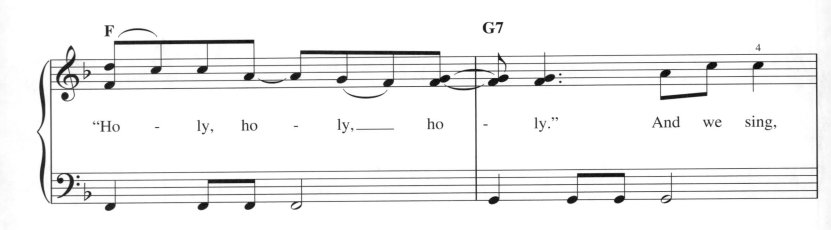

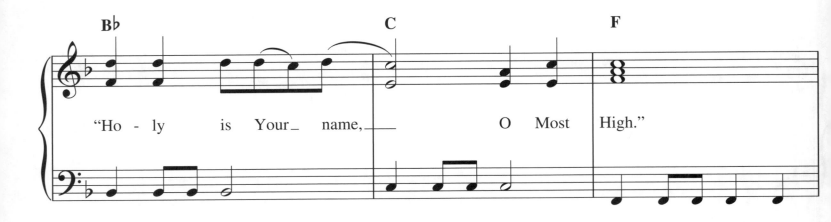

And Lord, please— haste— the day— when my

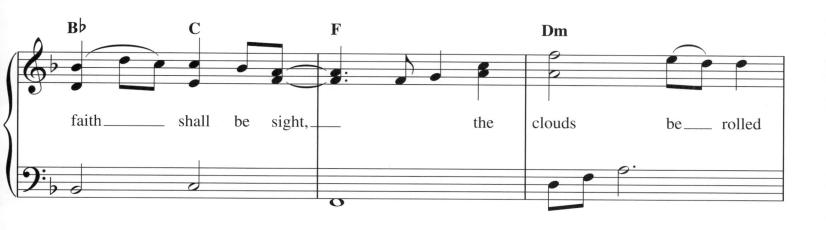

faith———— shall be sight,— the clouds be— rolled

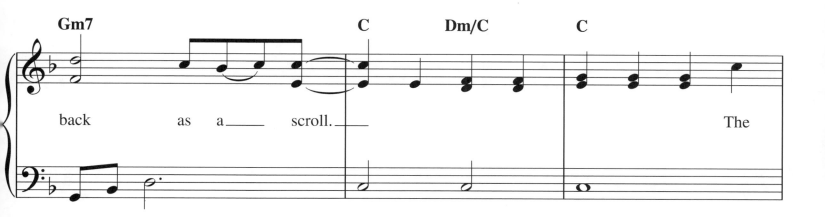

back as a— scroll.— The

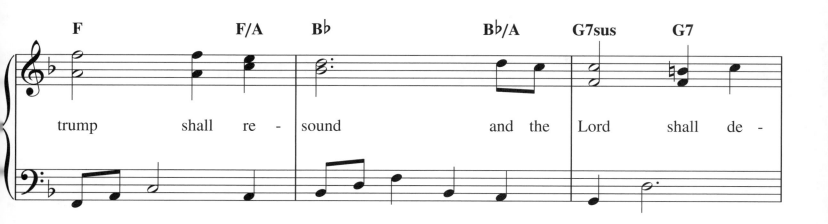

trump shall re - sound and the Lord shall de -

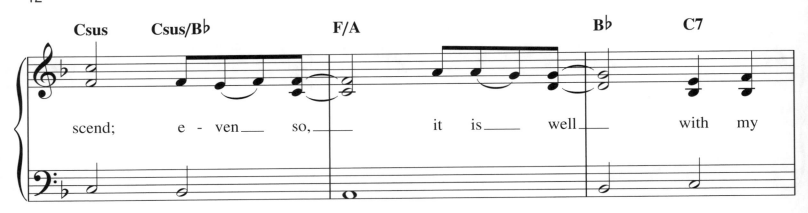

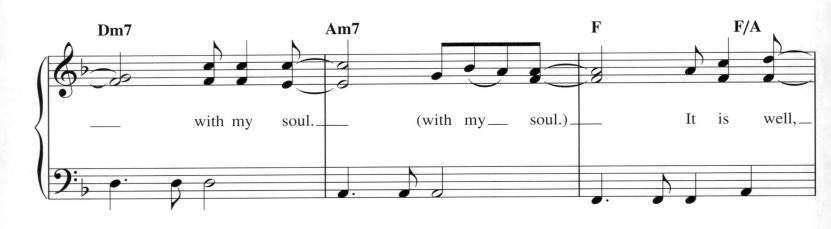

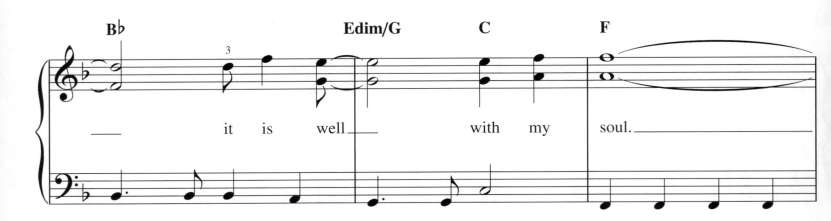

It is well___ (It is_____ well)_

___ with my soul.___ (with my_____ soul.)_

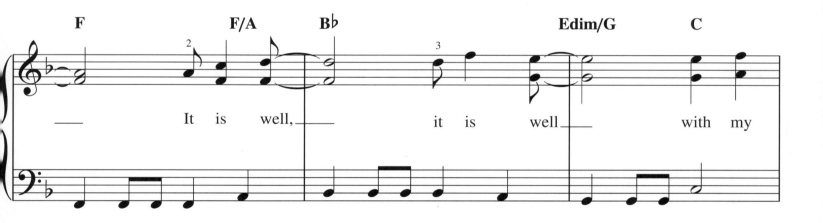

___ It is well,___ it is well___ with my

soul.

ALL CREATURES OF OUR GOD AND KING

Traditional
Arranged by CHRISTOPHER STEVENS

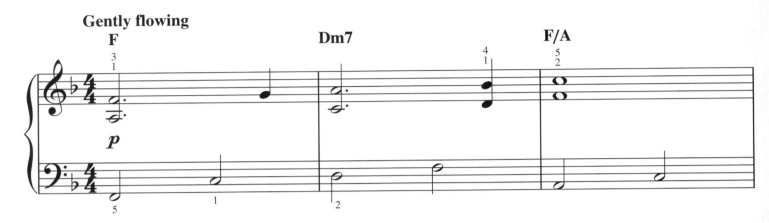

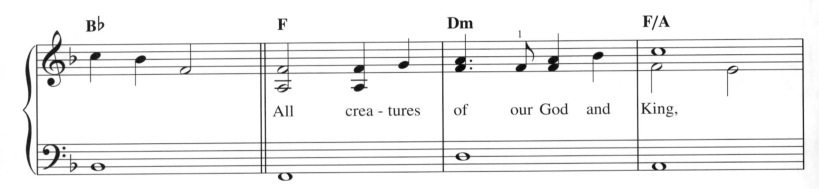

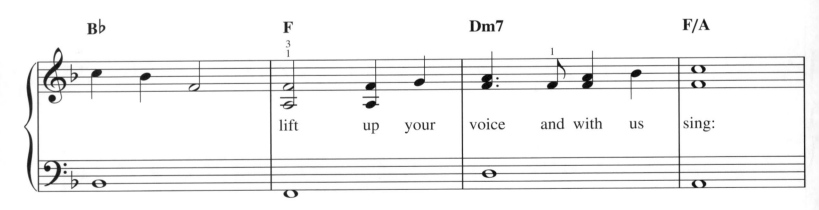

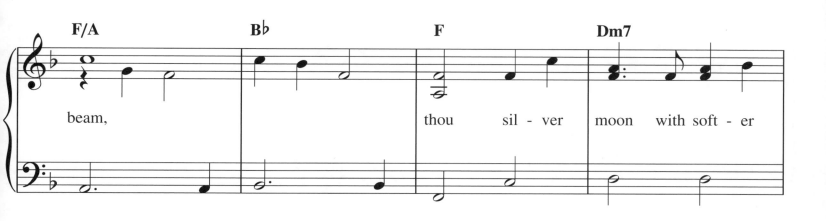

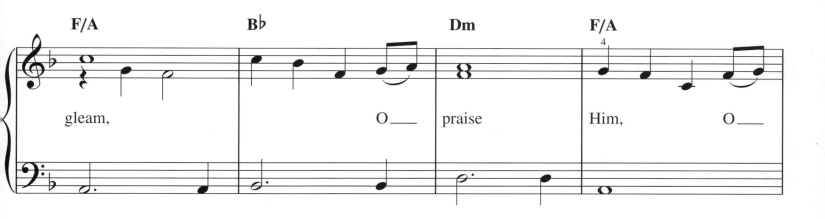

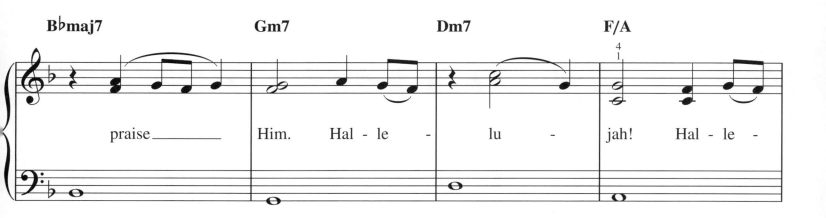

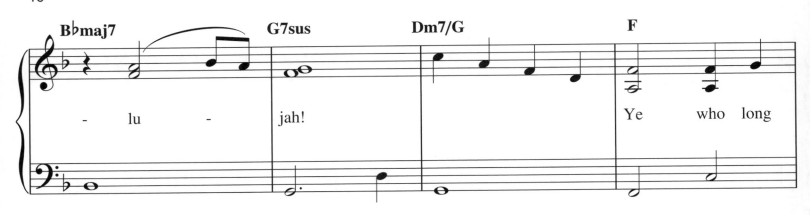

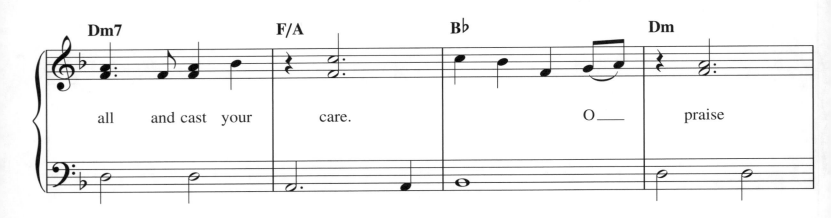

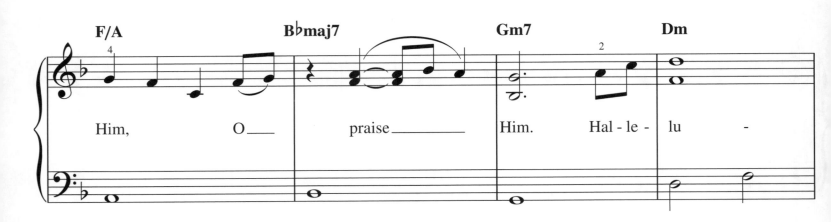

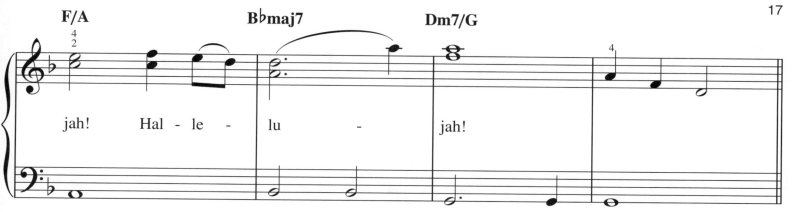

jah! Hal - le - lu - jah!

Moderately

Rush-ing wind that art so strong, clouds that sail in Heav'n a - long, ris-ing morn in praise re -

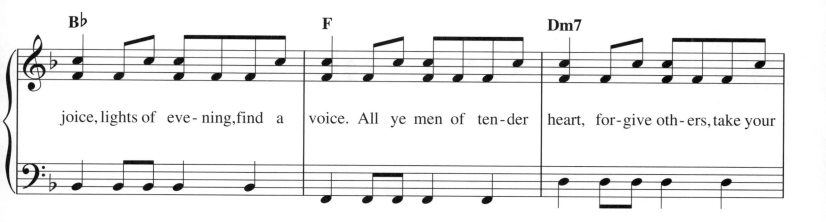

joice, lights of eve-ning, find a voice. All ye men of ten-der heart, for-give oth-ers, take your

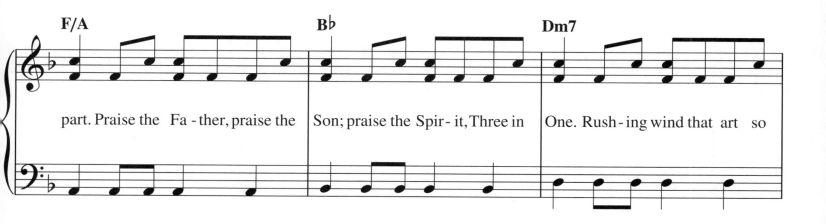

part. Praise the Fa - ther, praise the Son; praise the Spir-it, Three in One. Rush-ing wind that art so

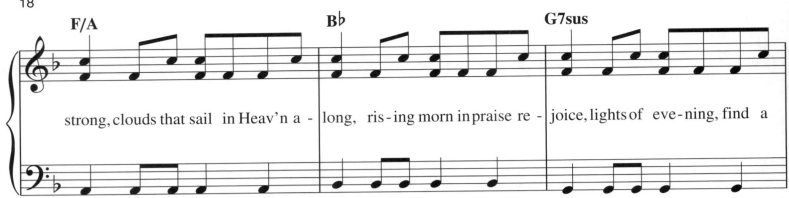

strong, clouds that sail in Heav'n a - long, ris - ing morn in praise re - joice, lights of eve - ning, find a

voice. All ye men of ten - der heart, for - give oth - ers, take your part. Praise the Fa - ther, praise the

Son; praise the Spir - it, Three in One. Hal - le - lu - jah! Hal - le - lu - jah!

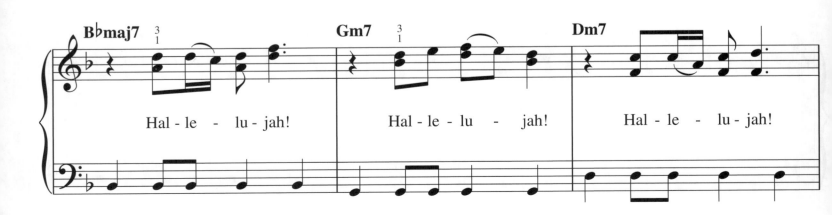

Hal - le - lu - jah! Hal - le - lu - jah! Hal - le - lu - jah!

Hal - le - lu - jah!   Hal - le - lu - jah!   Hal - le - lu - jah!

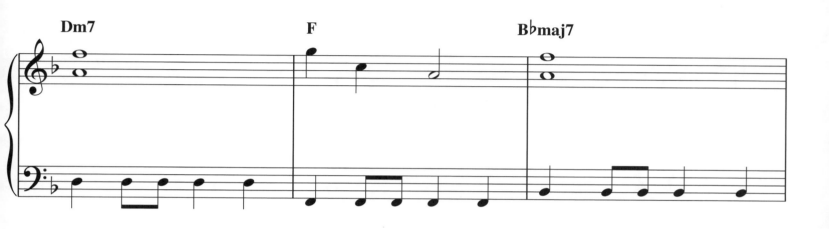

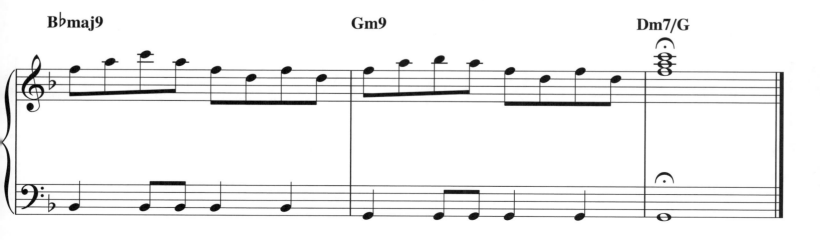

HOLY, HOLY, HOLY

Traditional
Arranged by STEVEN CURTIS CHAPMAN

Holy, ho - ly, ho - ly,   Lord God Al -
Ho - ly, ho - ly, ho - ly,   though the dark - ness

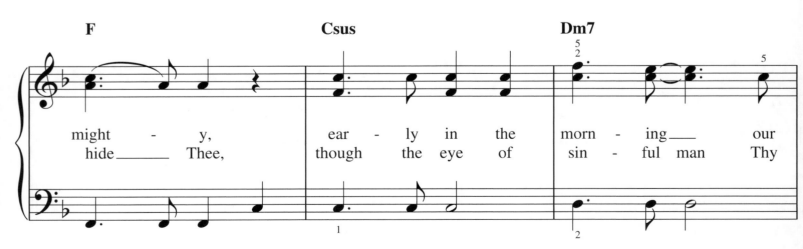

might - y,   ear - ly in the morn - ing____ our
hide____ Thee,   though the eye of sin - ful man Thy

song shall rise to Thee.
glo - ry may not see.

Ho - ly, ho - ly,
On - ly Thou art

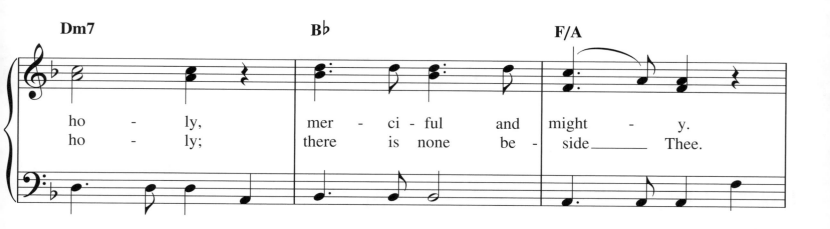

ho - ly,
ho - ly;

mer - ci - ful and
there is none be -

might - y.
side_____ Thee.

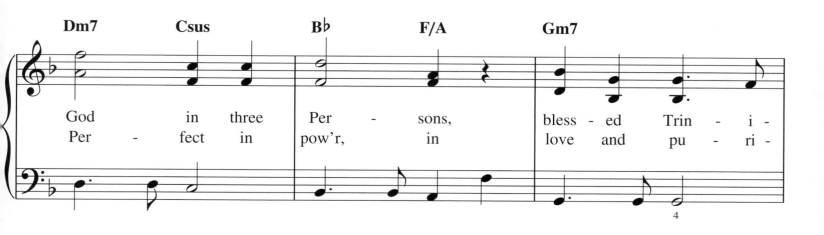

God in three
Per - fect in

Per - sons,
pow'r, in

bless - ed Trin - i -
love and pu - ri -

1.

ty.

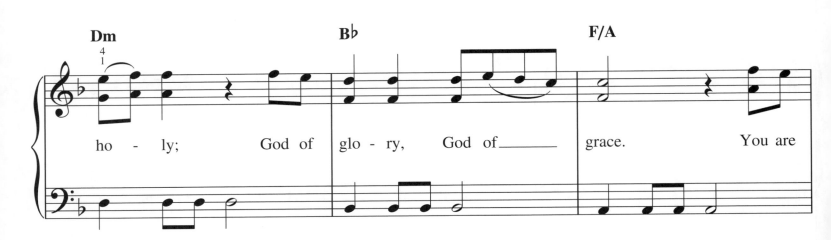

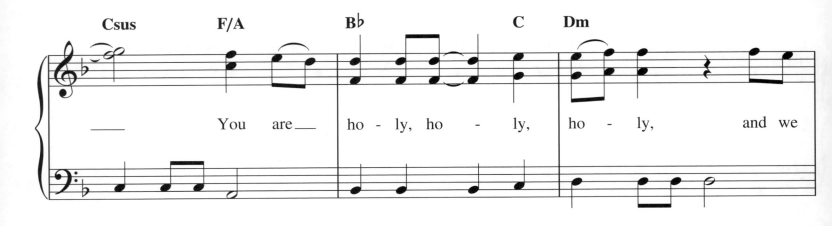

bow be - fore You____ now.   We're sing-ing, "Ho - ly,____

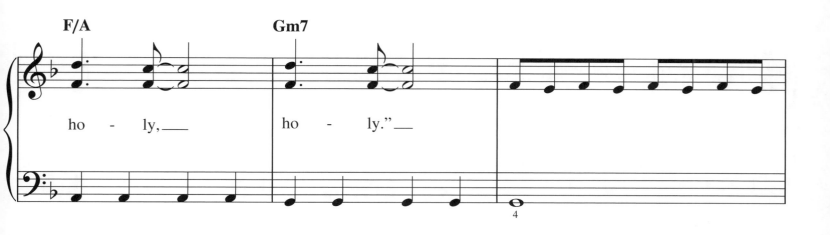

ho - ly,____   ho - ly."____

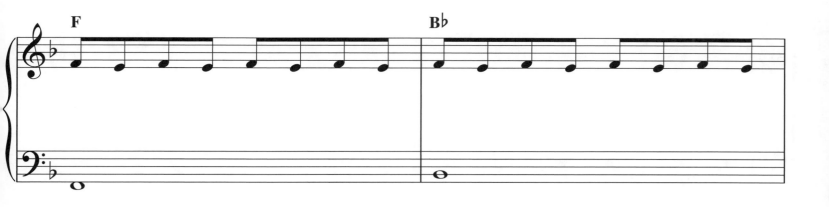

Ho - ly, ho - ly, ho - ly,   Lord God Al -

24

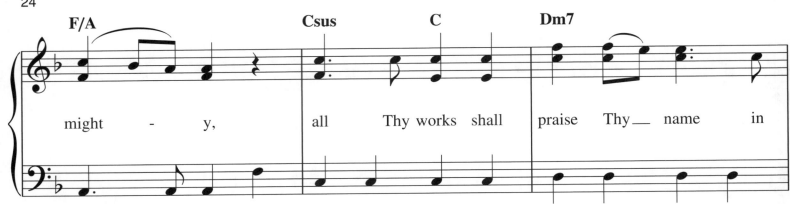

might - y, all Thy works shall praise Thy— name in

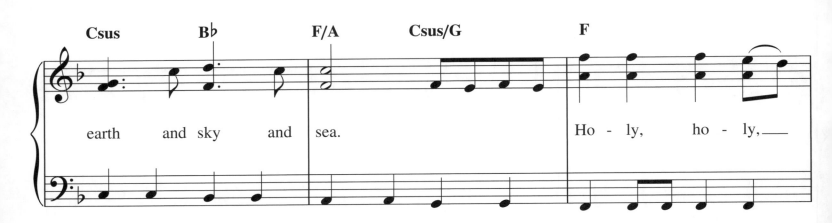

earth and sky and sea. Ho - ly, ho - ly,—

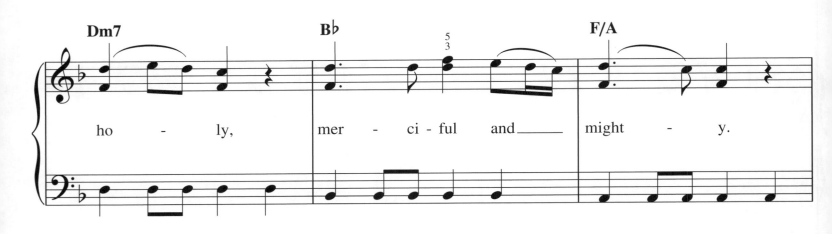

ho - ly, mer - ci - ful and— might - y.

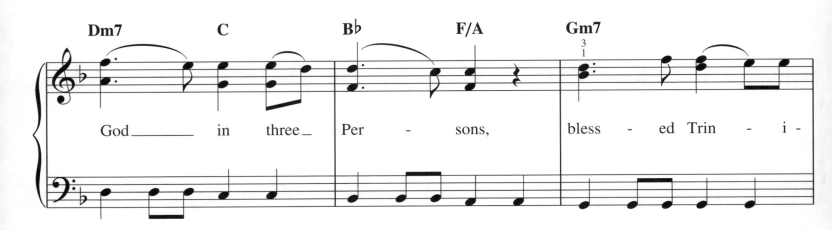

God— in three— Per - sons, bless - ed Trin - i -

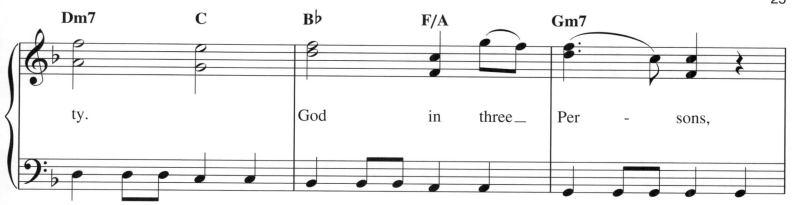

ty. God in three___ Per - sons,

bless - ed Trin - i - ty.

You are ho - ly. (Ho - ly, ho - ly,

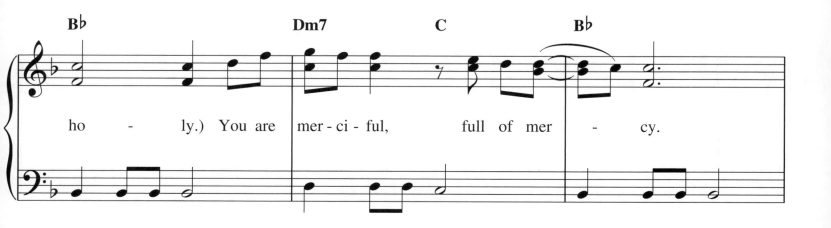

ho - ly.) You are mer - ci - ful, full of mer - cy.

26

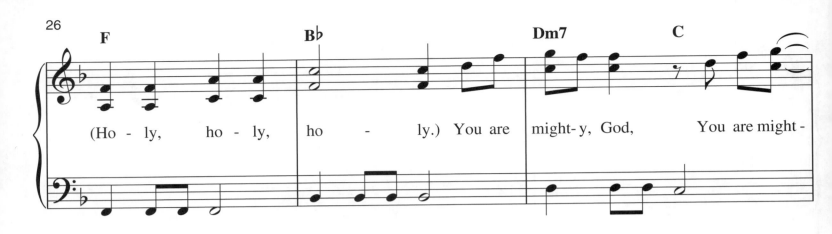

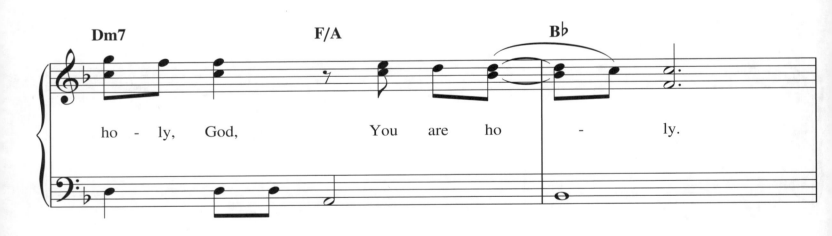

WERE YOU THERE?

Traditional
Arranged by SMOKIE NORFUL,
CEDRIC CALDWELL and VICTOR CALDWELL

Slowly, with freedom

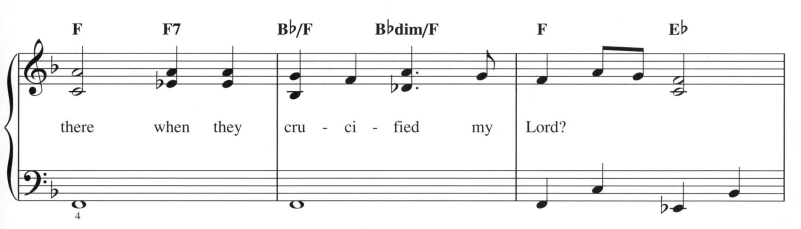

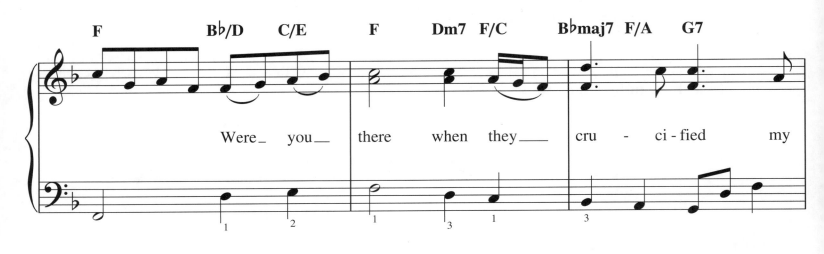

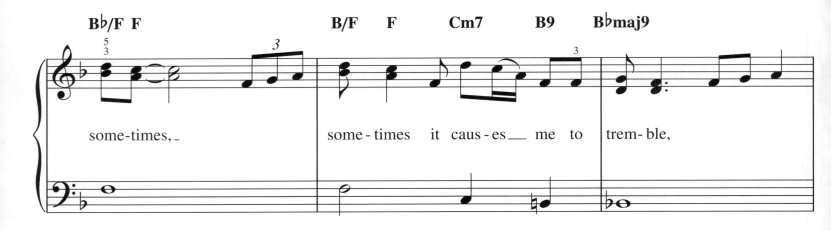

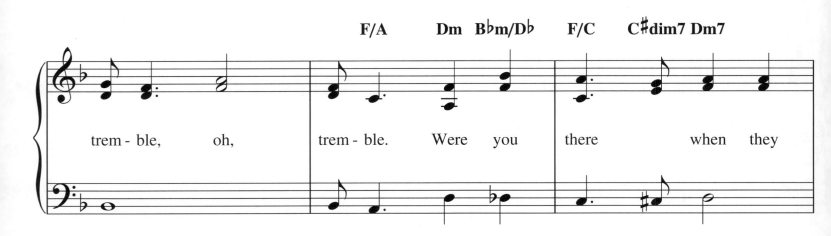

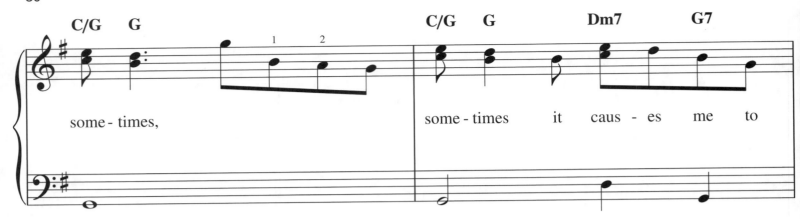

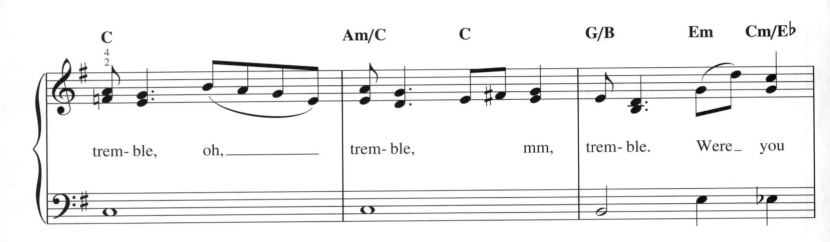

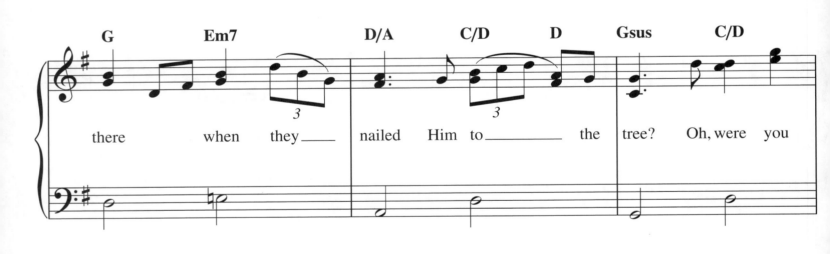

FAIREST LORD JESUS

Traditional
Arranged by JAMIE KENNEY
and BERNIE HERMS

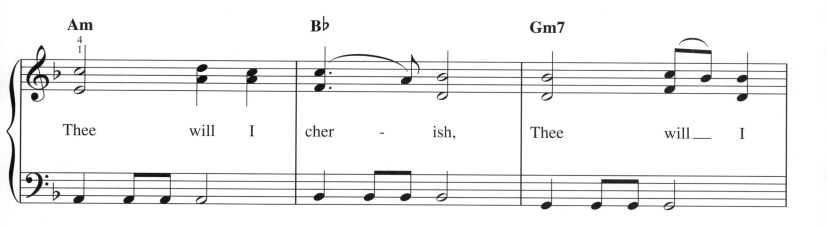

Thee will I cher - ish, Thee will I

hon - or, Thou my soul's glo - ry, joy and

crown.

Fair is the

sun - shine, fair - er still the moon - light,

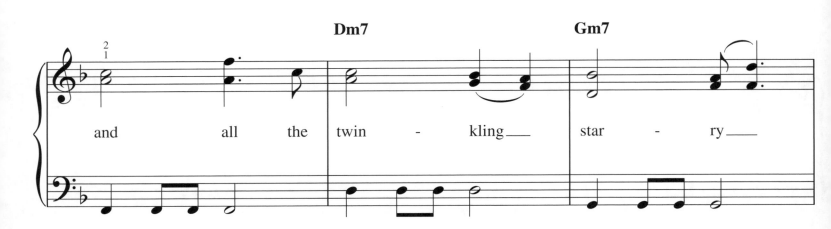

and all the twin - kling___ star - ry___

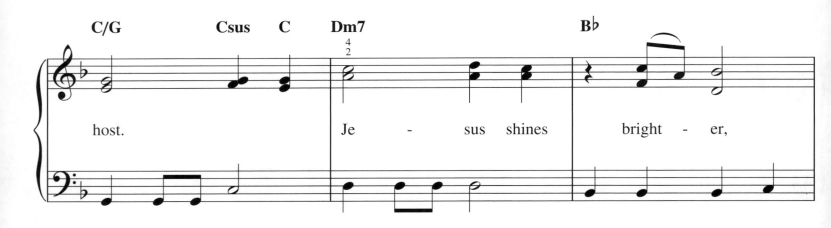

host. Je - sus shines bright - er,

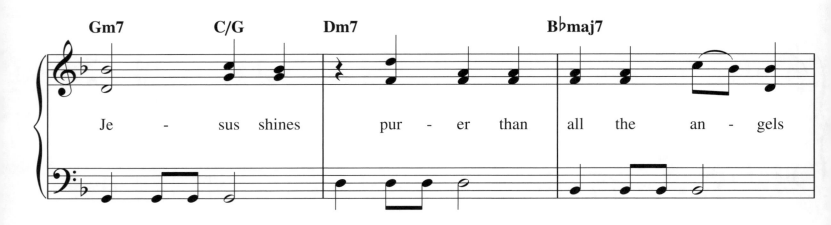

Je - sus shines pur - er than all the an - gels

heav - en can boast. ____ Oh, ____

oh, ____ oh, ____

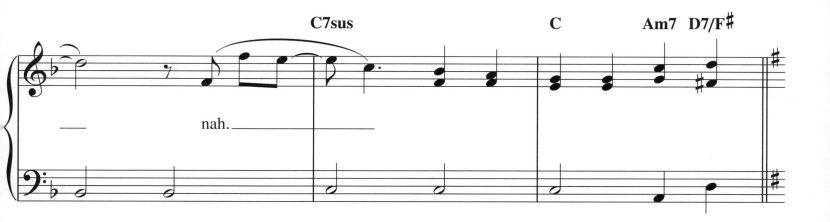

nah. ____

Beau - ti - ful Sav - ior, Lord of all the

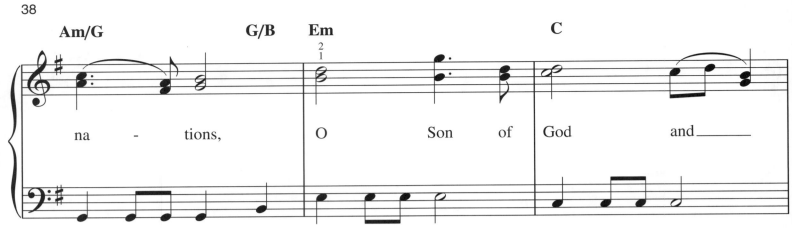

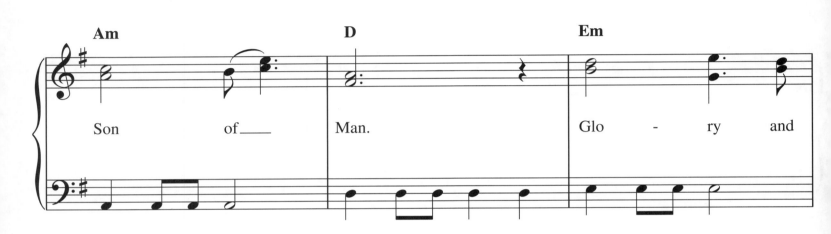

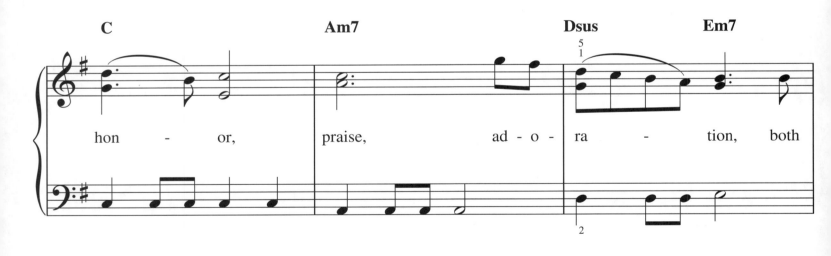

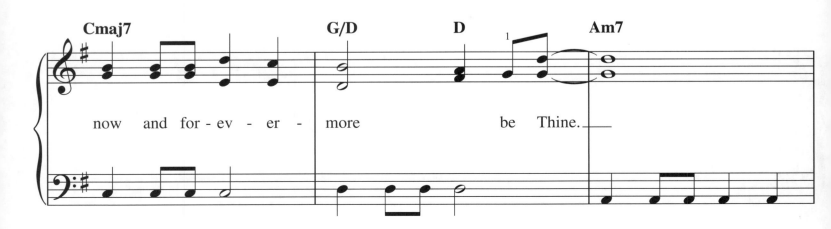

I NEED THEE EVERY HOUR

Words by ANNIE S. HAWKS
Music by ROBERT LOWRY
Additional Refrain and Bridge by CHARLIE LOWELL,
DAN HASELTINE, MATT ODMARK and STEPHEN MASON

42

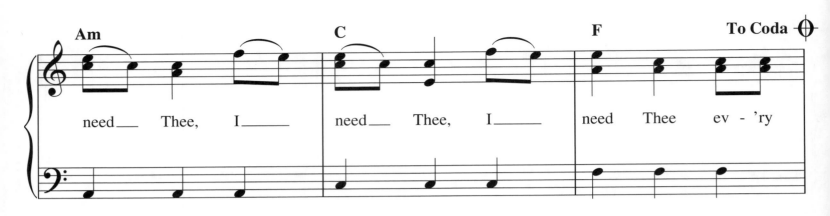

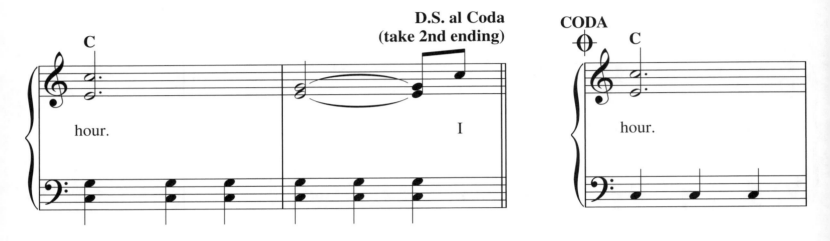

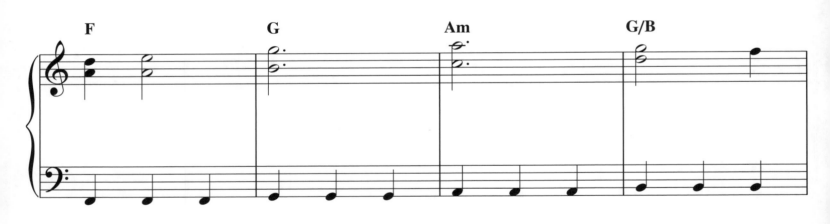

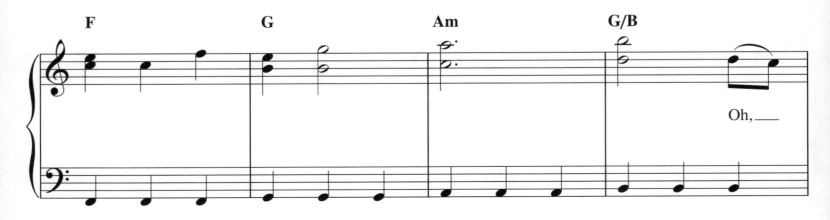

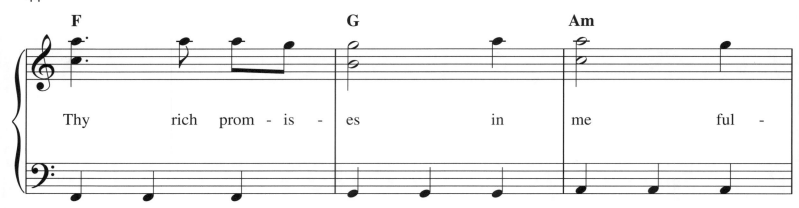

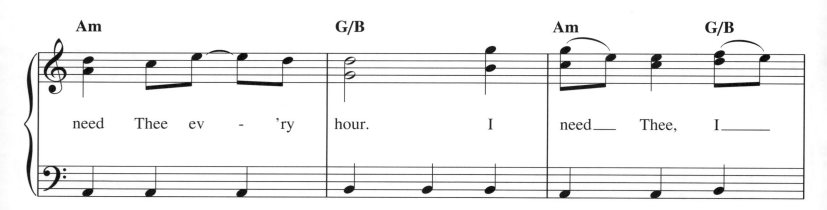

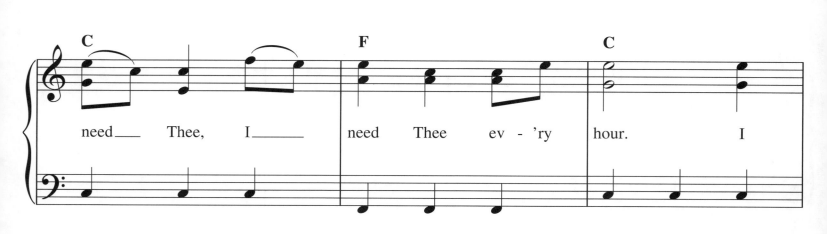

need Thee, I____ need Thee, I need___ Thee ev - 'ry

hour. I need___ Thee, I____ need___ Thee, I____

need Thee ev - 'ry hour. Oh, bless me now, my

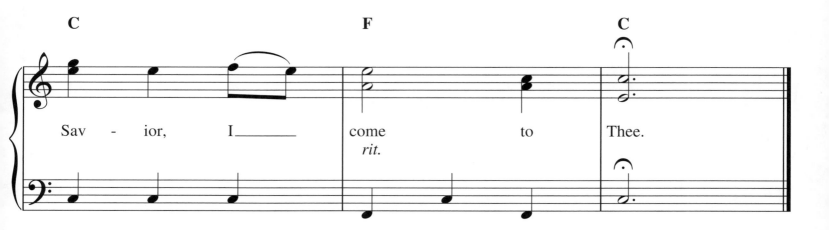

Sav - ior, I____ come to Thee.

rit.

JUST AS I AM

Traditional
New Verses by NICHOLE NORDEMAN

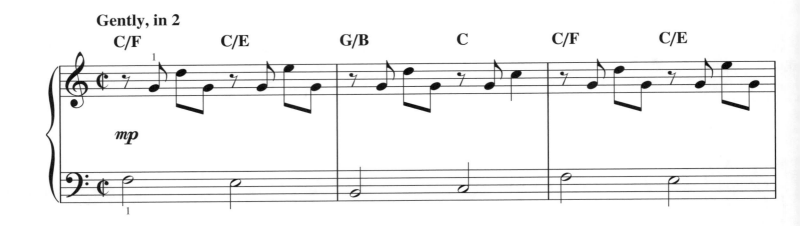

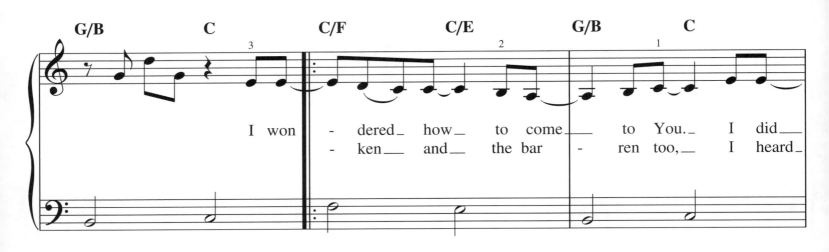

I won- dered_ how_ to come_ to You._ I did_
-ken_ and_ the bar - ren too,_ I heard_

_ not_ dare_ be - lieve_ it true_ that You re - gard_ the or-
_ could_ find_ some rest_ in You._ What kind of love_ in in-

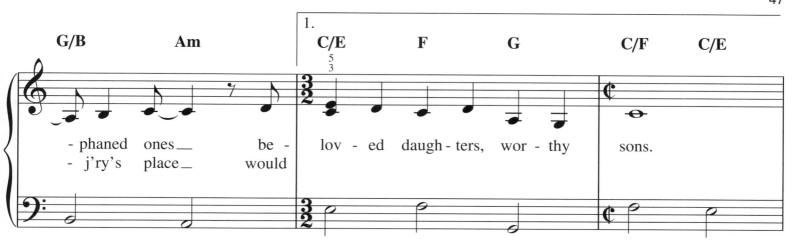

-phaned ones___ be- | lov-ed daugh-ters, wor-thy | sons.
-j'ry's place___ would

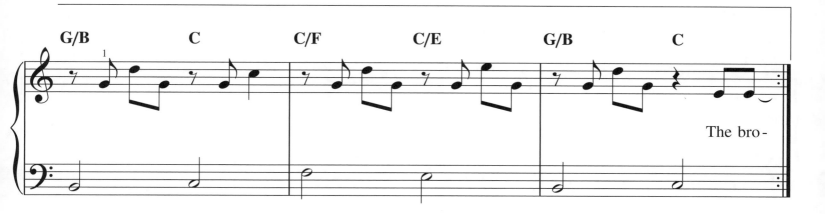

The bro-

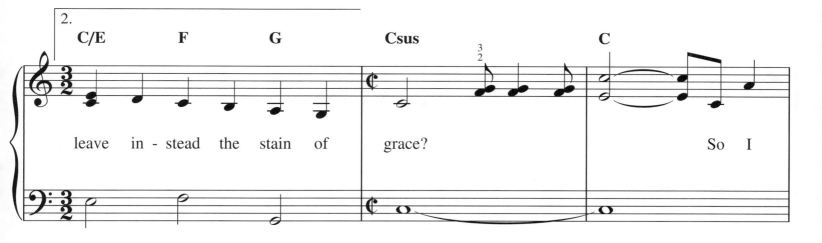

leave in-stead the stain of | grace? | So I

come_____ in sor- | row_____ and I | come_____ in shame,_

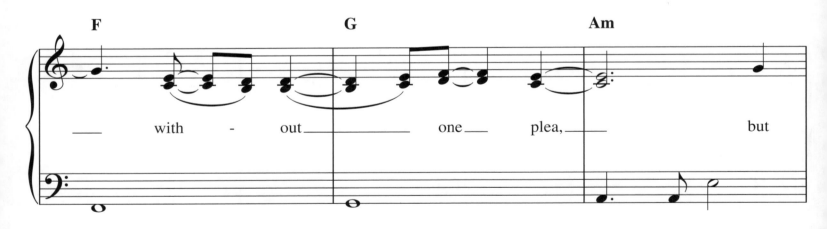

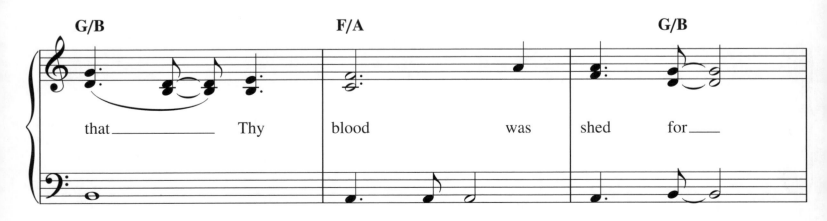

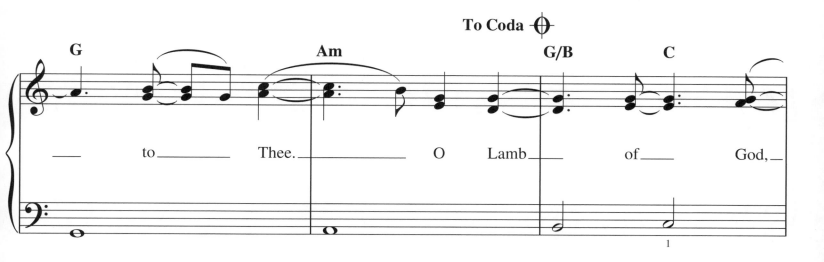

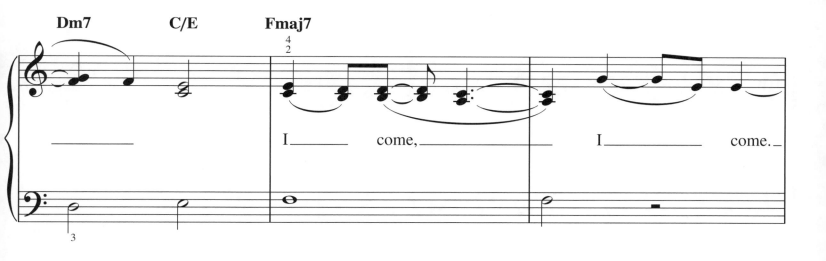

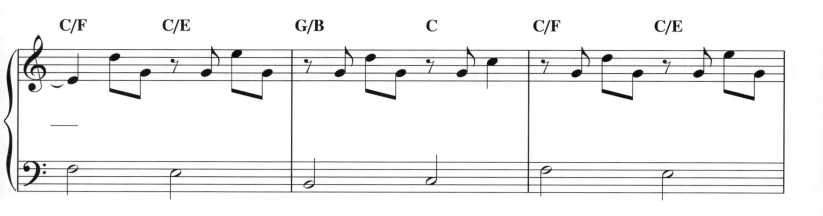

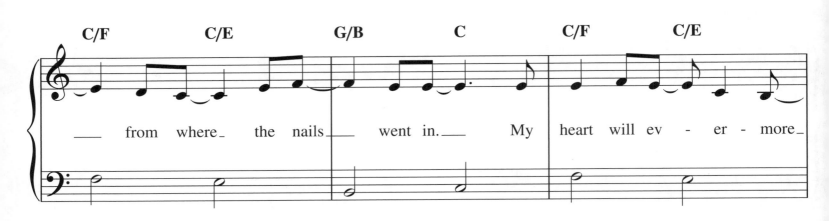

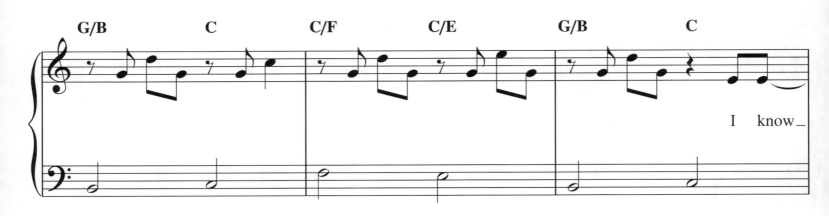

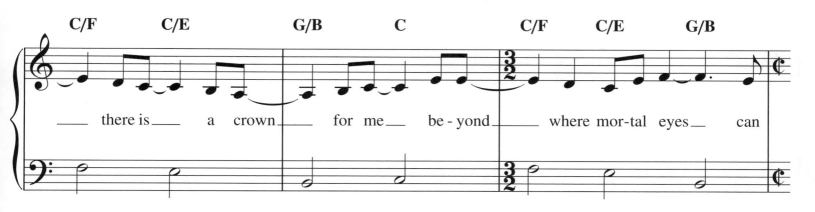

there is___ a crown___ for me___ be-yond___ where mor-tal eyes___ can

see.___ And I___ don't nod___ to an-

-y man,___ but of-fer me just as I am.

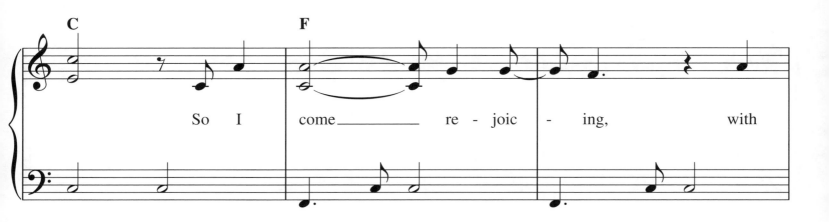

So I come___ re-joic-ing, with

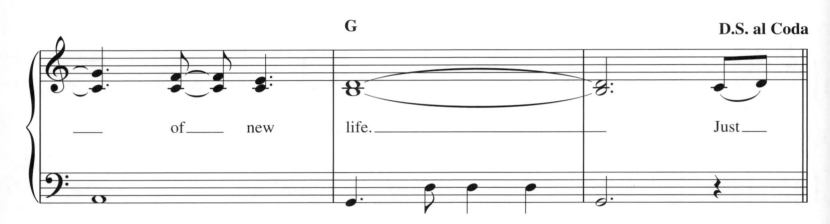

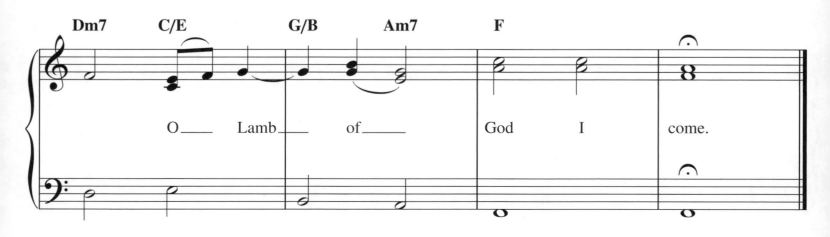

ROCK OF AGES

Words by AUGUSTUS M. TOPLADY
Music by THOMAS HASTINGS
Arranged by MARTY STUART

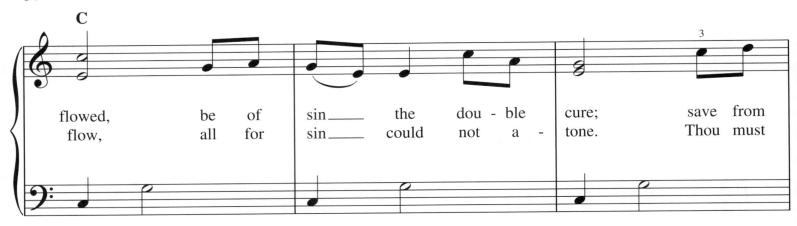

flowed, be of sin the dou - ble cure; save from
flow, all for sin could not a - tone. Thou must

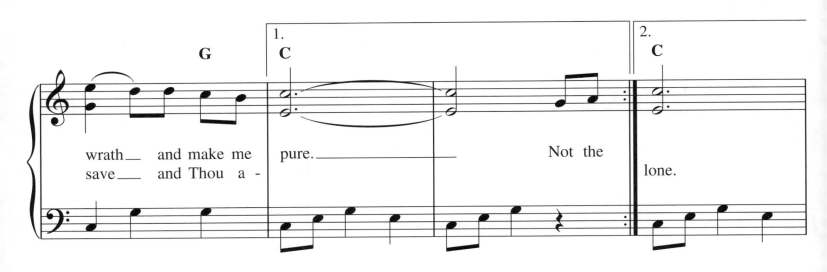

wrath and make me pure. Not the
save and Thou a - lone.

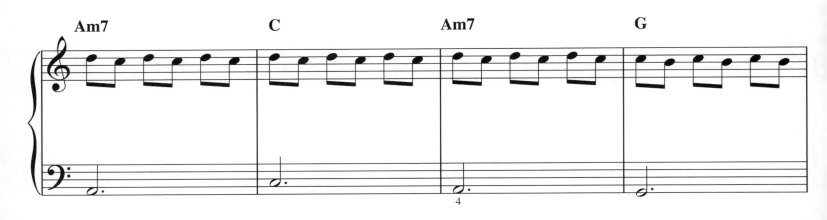

Noth - ing in my hand I bring; sim - ply

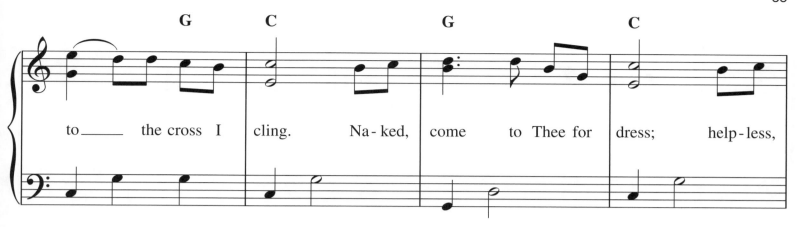

to_____ the cross I | cling. Na-ked, come | to Thee for dress; | help-less,

look to Thee for | grace. Foul, I | to_____ the foun-tain | fly. Wash me,

Sav - ior, or I | die. Foul, I | to the foun-tain | fly. Wash me,

Sav - ior, or I_____ | die._____

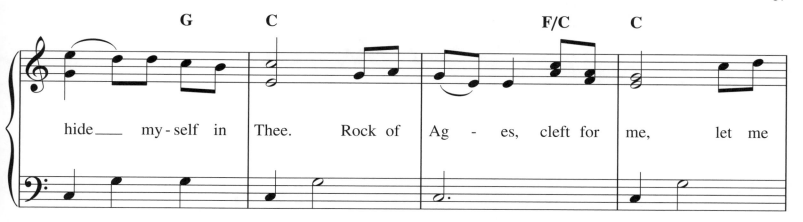

hide____ my-self in Thee. Rock of Ag - es, cleft for me, let me

hide____ my-self in Thee. Let me hide____ my-self in____ Thee._

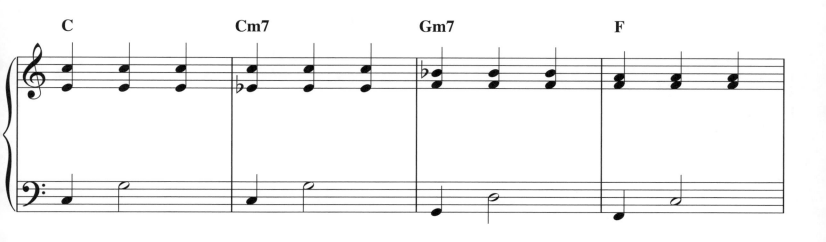

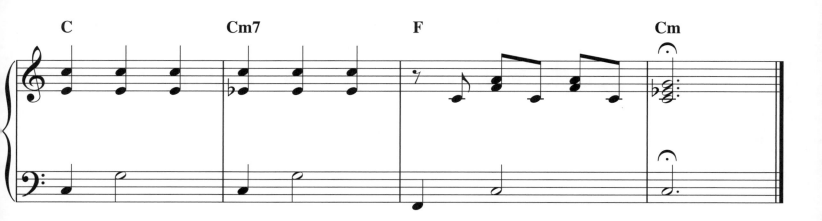

MY JESUS, I LOVE THEE/
'TIS SO SWEET

Words by WILLIAM R. FEATHERSTONE
Music by ADONIRAM J. GORDON

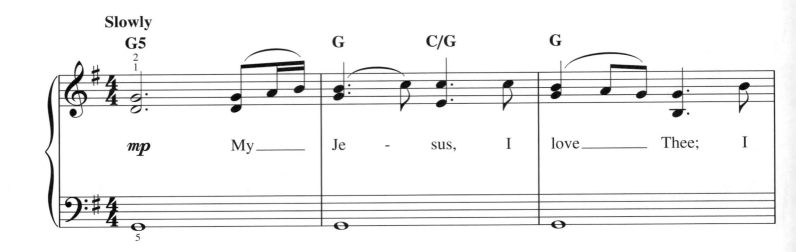

My ____ Je - sus, I love ____ Thee; I

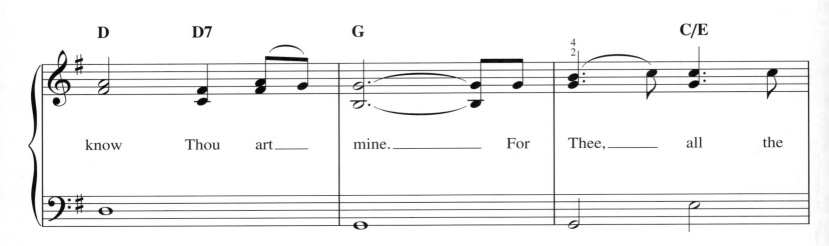

know Thou art ____ mine. ____ For Thee, ____ all the

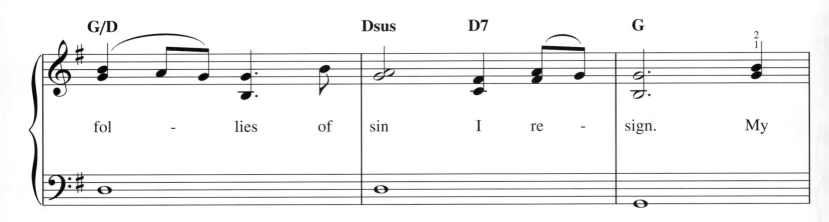

fol - lies of sin I re - sign. My

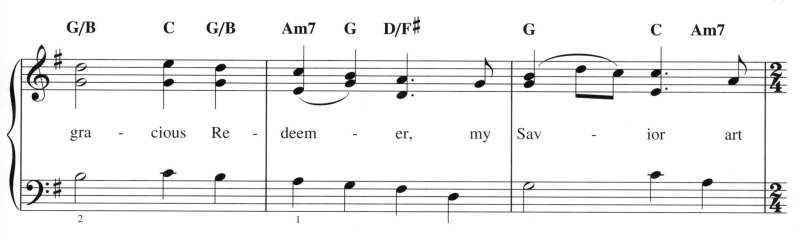

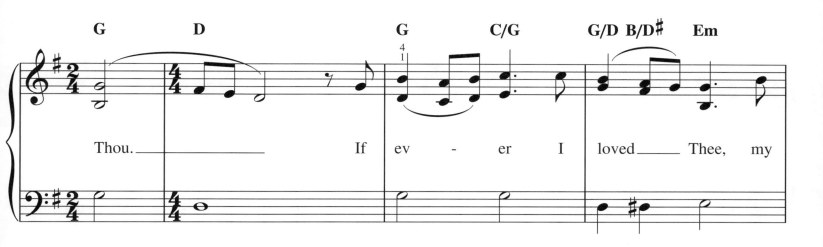

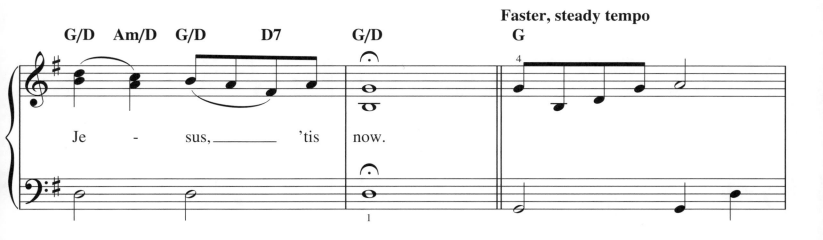

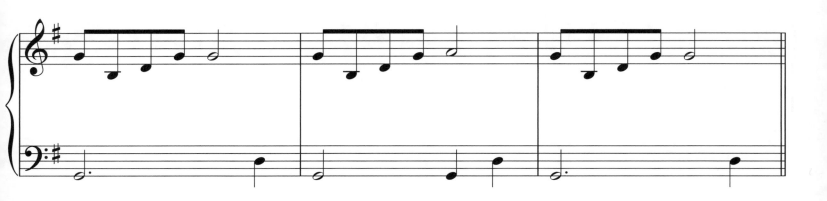

'TIS SO SWEET
Words by LOUISA M.R. STEAD
Music by WILLIAM KIRKPATRICK

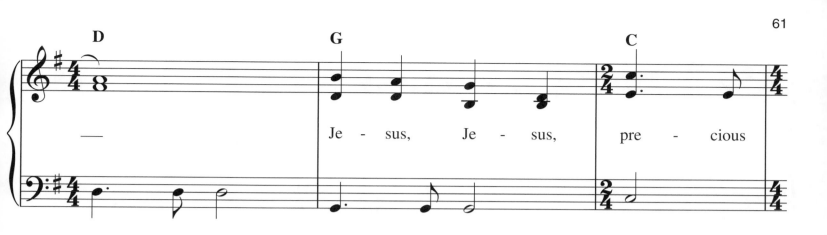

Je - sus, Je - sus, pre - cious

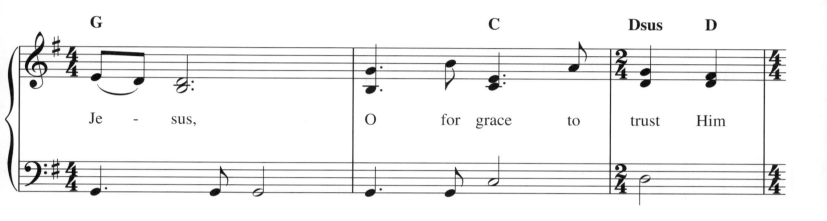

Je - sus, O for grace to trust Him

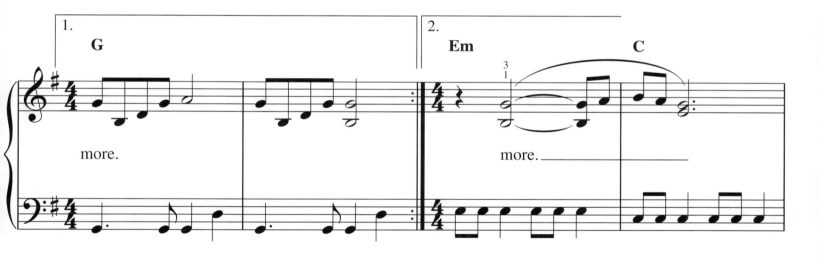

1. more.

2. more._____

We're gon-na trust You more._____ We're gon-na

trust You Lord.   We're gon-na   trust You Lord.

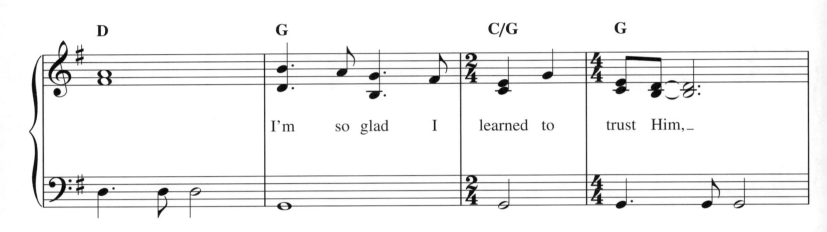

I'm   so glad   I   learned to   trust Him,

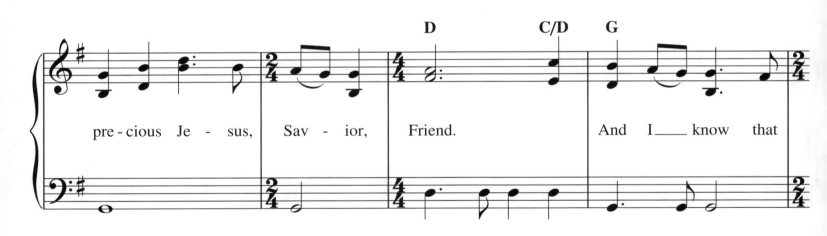

pre - cious Je - sus,   Sav - ior,   Friend.   And I___ know that

He   is   with me,___   will be with me   to the

63

GREAT IS THY FAITHFULNESS

Words by THOMAS O. CHISHOLM
Music by WILLIAM M. RUNYAN

Thou chang - est not, Thy com - pas - sions they

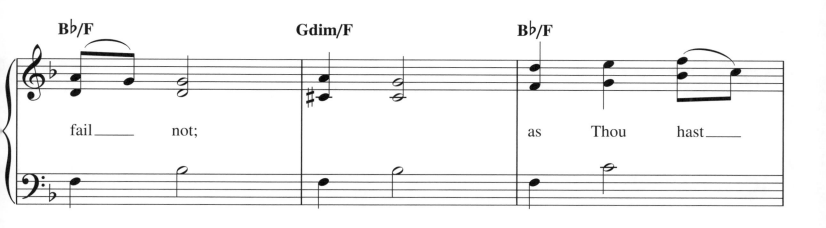

fail___ not; as Thou hast___

been, Thou for - ev - er will be.

Great is Thy faith - ful - ness,

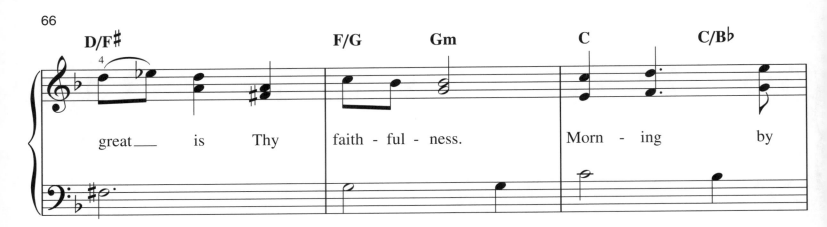

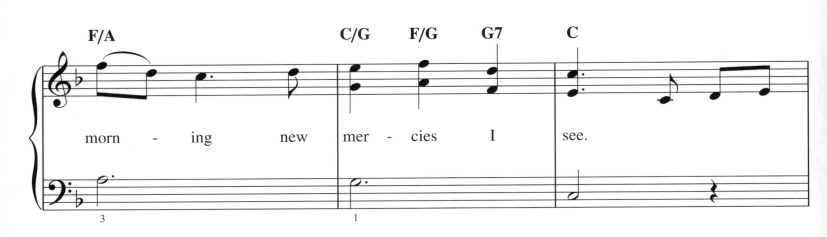

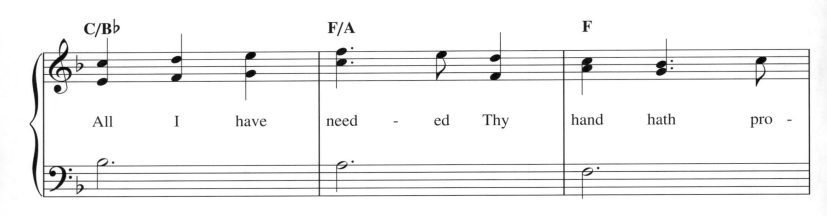

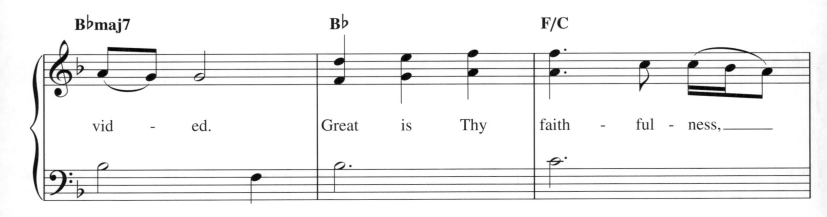

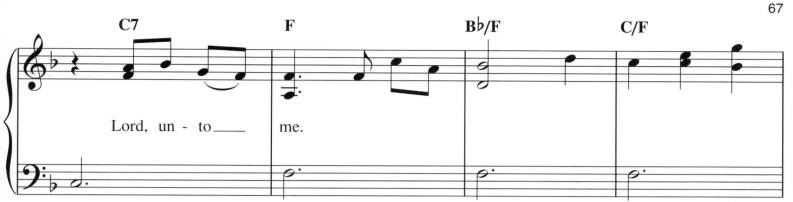

Lord, un - to___ me.

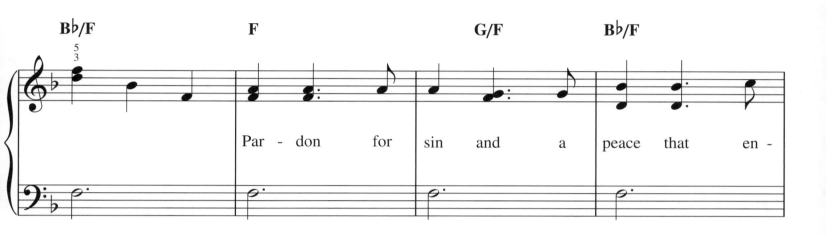

Par - don for sin and a peace that en -

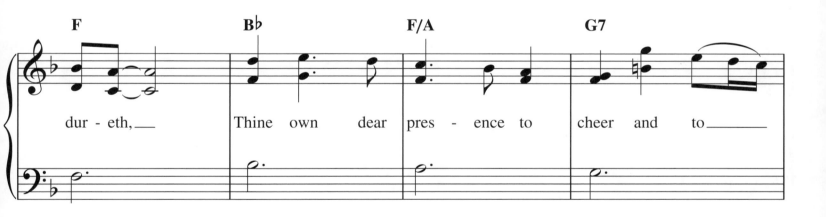

dur - eth,___ Thine own dear pres - ence to cheer and to___

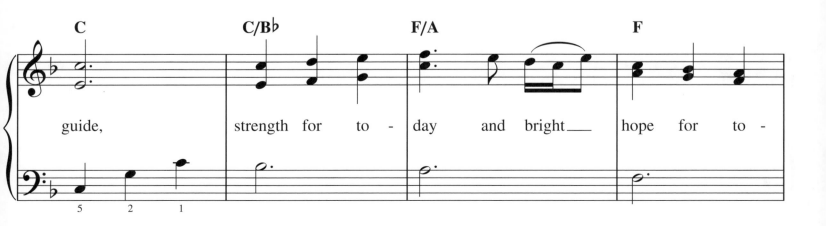

guide, strength for to - day and bright___ hope for to -

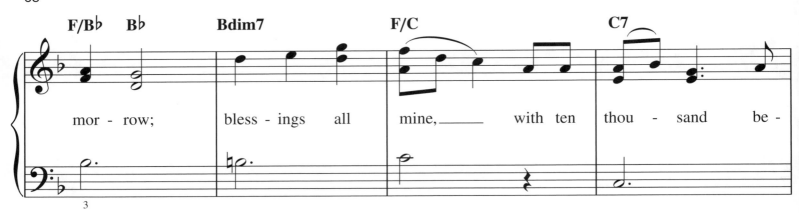

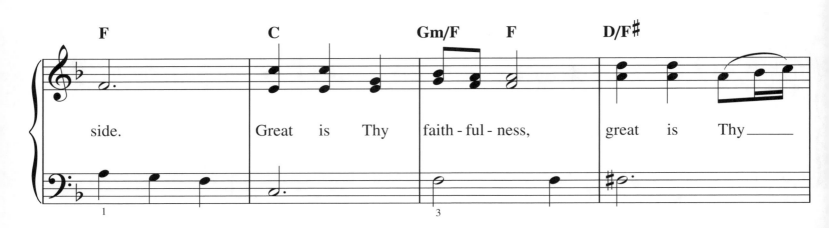

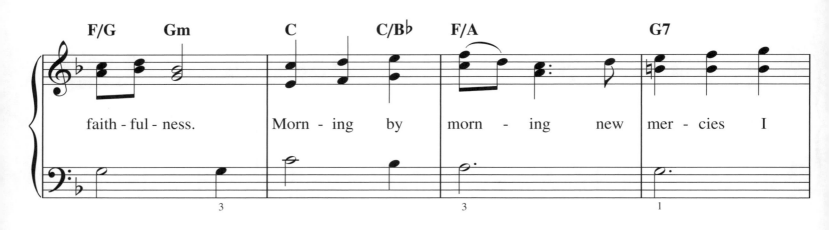

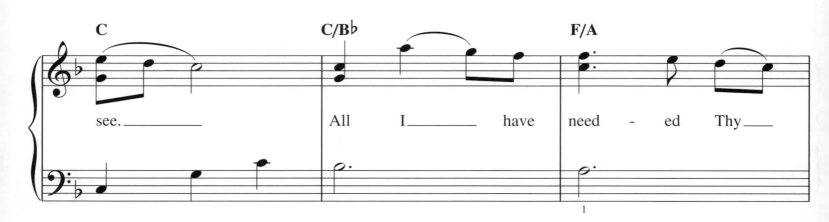

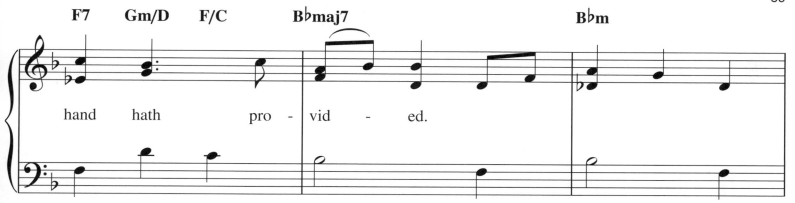

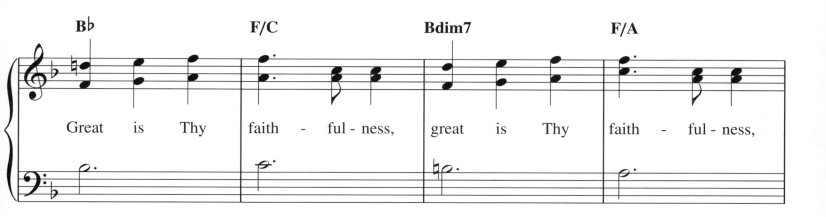

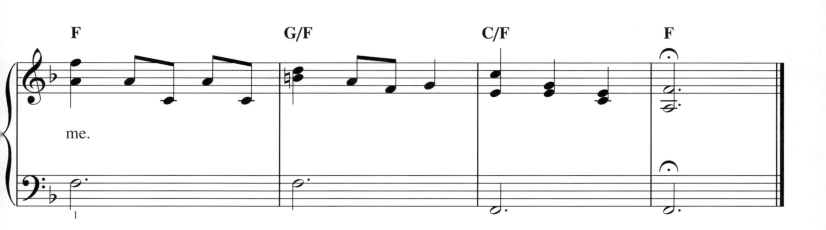

HOW GREAT THOU ART

Words and Music by
STUART K. HINE

*Author's original words are "works" and "mighty."

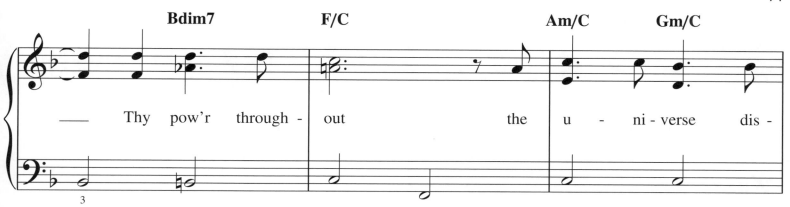

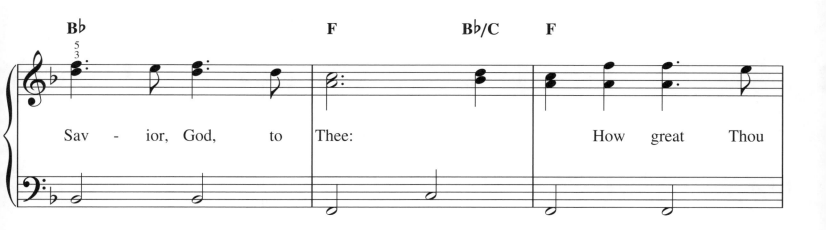

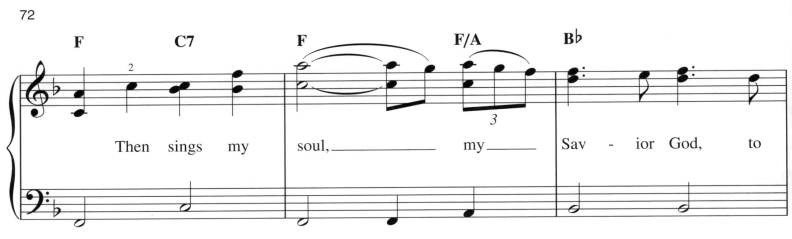

Then sings my soul,_____ my_____ Sav - ior God, to

Thee: How__ great Thou art,

how great Thou art!_____

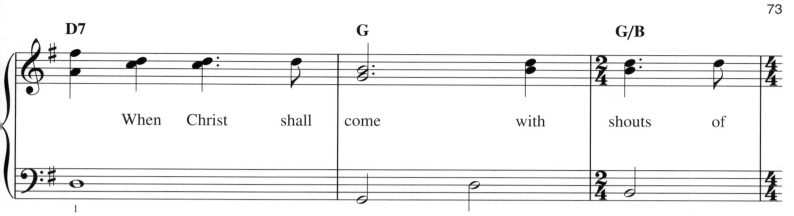

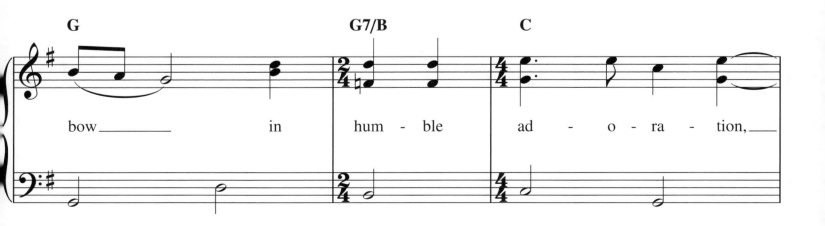

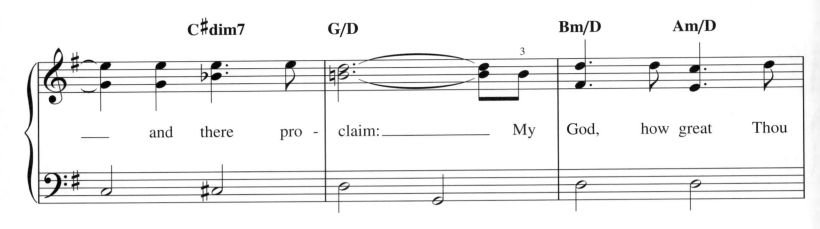

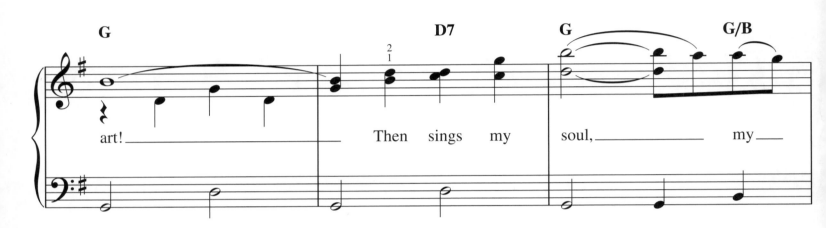

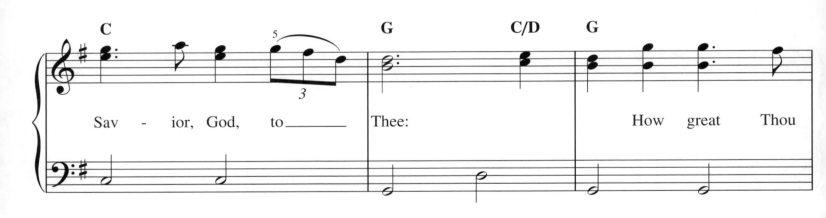

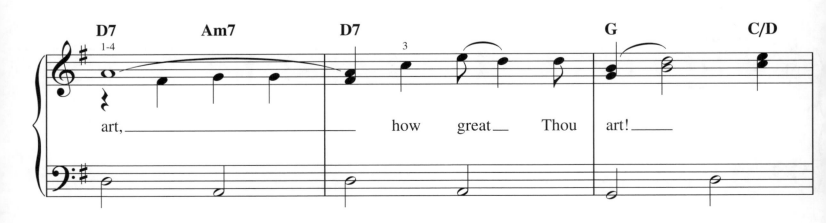

NEARER MY GOD TO THEE

Traditional
Arranged by CEDRIC CALDWELL
and VICTOR CALDWELL

Slowly, somewhat rubato

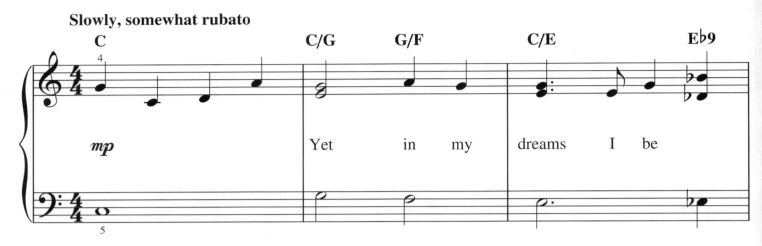

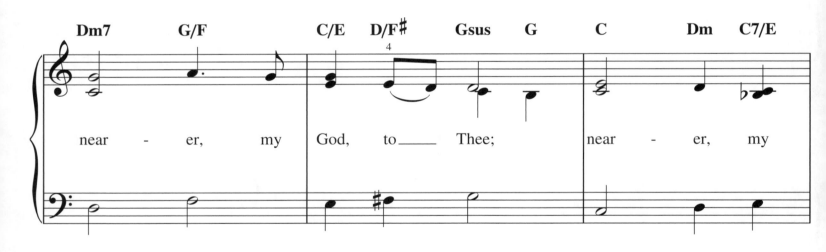

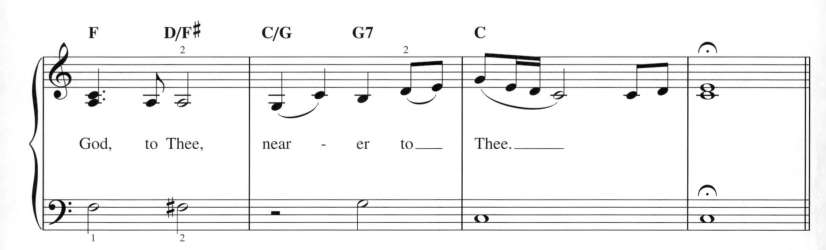

A little faster

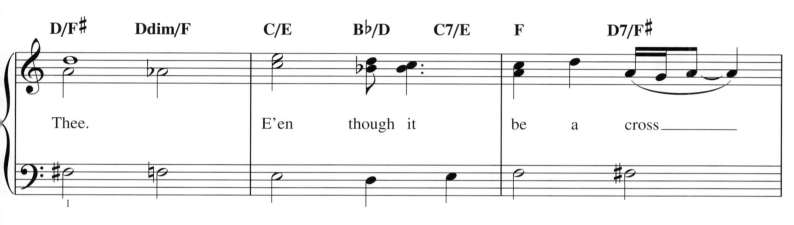

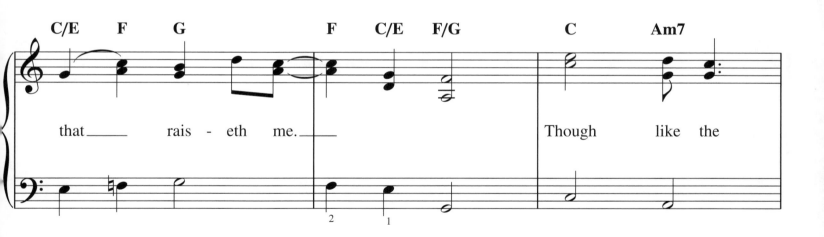

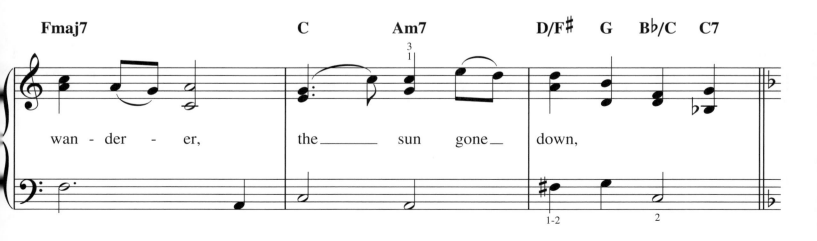

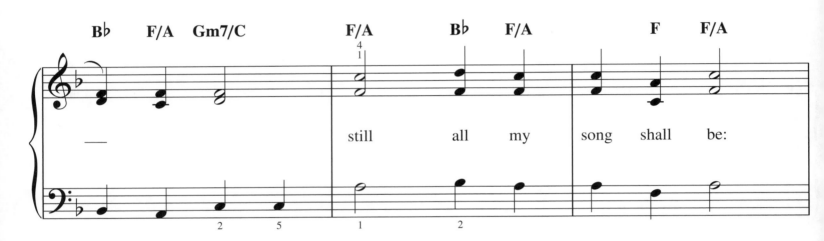

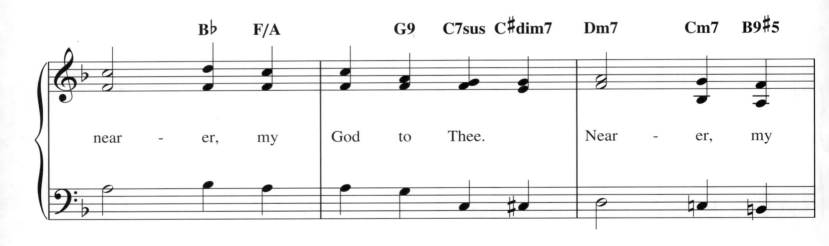

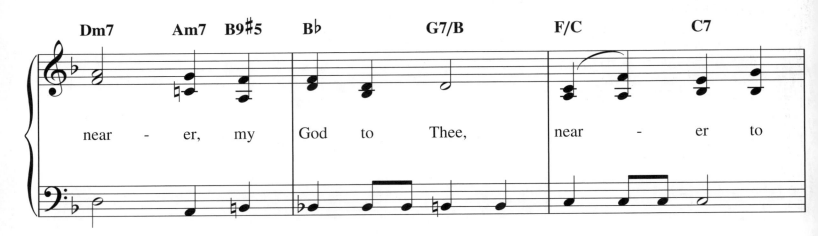

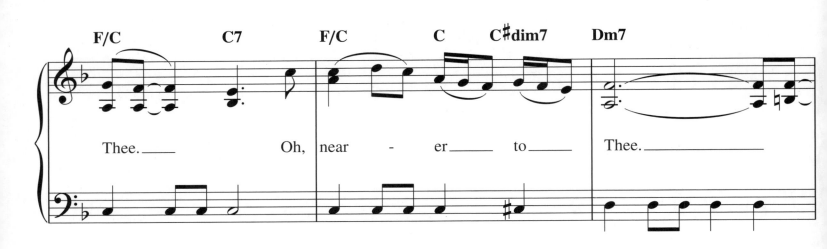

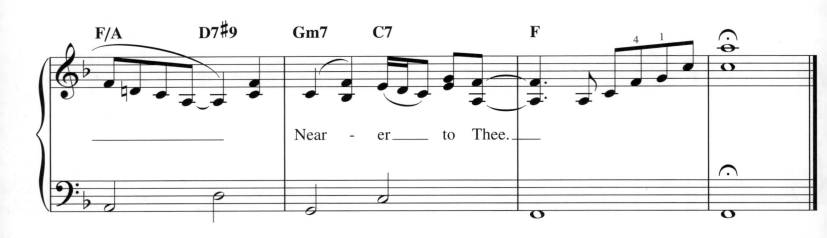